# 563 Stupid Things People Do to Mess Up Their Lives

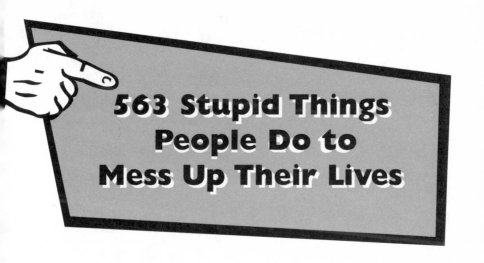

# 563 Stupid Things People Do to Mess Up Their Lives

## Dr. Larry

Thomas Dunne Books

St. Martin's Griffin ≋ New York

THOMAS DUNNE BOOKS.
An imprint of St. Martin's Press.

563 STUPID THINGS PEOPLE DO TO MESS UP THEIR LIVES. Copyright © 2000 by Larry
Samuel. All rights reserved. Printed in the United States of America. No part of this
book may be used or reproduced in any manner whatsoever without written permission
except in the case of brief quotations embodied in critical articles
or reviews. For information, address St. Martin's Press, 175 Fifth Avenue,
New York, N.Y. 10010.

ISBN 0-312-25279-X

First Edition: April 2000

10   9   8   7   6   5   4   3   2   1

# CONTENTS

*vi*

## ACKNOWLEDGMENTS

Through my private practice, national radio show, and syndicated newspaper column I have the good fortune of meeting thousands of people from all walks of life. I am therefore in the very fortunate position of being, if I may say so, an expert in the dynamics of stupidity. I take it as my responsibility, if not my obligation, to pass on my knowledge of all things stupid to you readers. *563 Stupid Things People Do to Mess Up Their Lives* would not have been possible without the generosity of those who came forth with their personal stories of stupidity in the hope that others do not repeat the same mistakes. I therefore dedicate this book to these unselfish yet still stupid souls whose benevolence will, I hope, help to make the world a less stupid place.

## INTRODUCTION

These are a few of my favorite stupid things people do to mess up their lives. The purpose of this book is to point out what I believe to be the more stupid of the stupid things people do in the hope that after reading it some readers will lead less messed-up lives. As I explained in my previous books, *What the Hell Were You Thinking?*, *How Could You Eat That?*, *Why Mediocre Things Happen to Mediocre People*, and *You Can't Spell Stupid Without U and I*, it is critical that one take responsibility for one's stupid actions. Too many of my colleagues out there allow the stupidity-inclined to get off the hook by blaming others or using the excuse that one was just in a particularly stupid frame of mind. Not Dr. Larry! I wholeheartedly believe that being accountable for one's stupidity is the best way to get on the road less stupid and, ultimately, avoid emotional and physical pain, financial ruin, and short- and long-term detainment by the legal system.

This book is the culmination of a career spent working with thousands of people to make stupidity a less prevalent force in their lives. Even before graduating from La Casa de la Grande Psicología in Guadalupe, Mexico, I realized my special calling was to work in the much ignored and often misunderstood area of stupidity management. Rather than set up shop in some fancy office on Madison Avenue, I dedicated myself to helping people from all social and economic backgrounds develop nonstupid life skills. (I'm a firm believer that stupidity is an equal opportunity condition, refusing to discriminate by race, gender, class, or any other demographic status.) *563 Stupid Things People Do to Mess Up Their Lives* is thus an extension of my mission, a wonderful opportunity to make thousands more individuals aware of their own personal stupidity and offer useful strategies for readers to lead a life less stupid.

Anyone who is not familiar with me, Dr. Larry, should be warned that I do not subscribe to classical psychology theories or traditional approaches to therapy. I do not believe that dysfunctional behavior is a result of deeply rooted psychoses, repressed memories, or envies of a particular bodily organ. Instead I believe that dysfunctional behavior is a result of an individual's brain performing at less than full capacity, a nice way of saying that this person has taken up temporary or permanent residence in Stupidville. This real-world versus theoretical view is gradually gaining steam as more of the psychological establishment recognizes the significant and, unfortunately for some, dominant role that stupidity plays in people's lives. It is my dream that more practicing mental healthcare workers embrace stupidity so that our collective future is a little less stupid than our decidedly stupid present and past.

When I began this book, I intended to focus on just a handful of stupid things people do to mess up their lives. I quickly realized, however, that there were many more stupid things than I originally believed, each one of them deserving of attention. Personal accounts of stupidity poured onto my desk and through the airwaves, raising my awareness of how much stupidity was actually out there in the real world. A handful quickly became one hundred, and before you could say stupid is as stupid does, I had amassed hundreds of stupid things that people do to mess up their lives. Each of these stupid things is—and this is an important point—stupid in its own unique way, although the core of every one remains stupidity.

The breadth of stupidity, I think you will agree when you read this book, is quite amazing. Stupidity is everywhere you look these days, invading every nook and cranny of society. Rather than focus on relationships or self-development, which most of my colleagues do, I take a much broader approach, believing that stupidity can be found in virtually every dimension of everyday life. Consider this book to be a bible of stupidity, a seminal resource of all things stupid in careers, relationships, spirituality, emotions, appearance, decisions, taste, traits, and many other areas. While not every example of stupidity will be relevant to you,

I am sure you will see yourself in many of these stupid things people do to mess up their lives. I myself am guilty of a number of them, but I have become less stupidity-inclined by confronting the stupidity within. I hope you do the same.

—Dr. Larry
New York City, September 1999

# 563 Stupid Things
# People Do to
# Mess Up Their Lives

# Stupid Achievements

How does one measure achievement when it is such a deeply personal concept? One way is to determine whether that which you hope to achieve is truly worth pursuing or is instead one of your patented exercises in stupidity. We all want recognition and praise for our actions, but if not careful we end up exposing ourselves to physical harm or what's worse, scorn and derision from our closest friends and loved ones. Here are some examples of achievements that Dr. Larry considers to fall on the decidedly stupid end of the stupidity scale.

### Achieve nirvana.
You've realized a state of pure and absolute blessedness, ecstasy, and bliss. Now what?

### Appear on cable-access television.
You must have a particularly stupid personal agenda if cable access is the only media vehicle that will have you. Channeling Mother Earth at 3 A.M. on channel 76b is not something you should be proud of.

**Be featured on *America's Most Wanted*.**
I would not consider being featured on this particular show a personal victory, despite the accepted tenet that any publicity is good publicity.

**Bend spoons with your mind.**
You can barely bend spoons with your hands, and you want to bend them with that head of cauliflower you call a brain? Do not attempt mind over matter when matter is clearly superior to your mind.

**Burp at will.**
Doing one thing and doing it very well is wise in most cases, but this is not one of them. This might have curried you favor as a youngster but will fail to win over many new acquaintances as an adult.

**Have an all-you-can-eat buffet named after you.**
While you should be proud of this at some level, your primary takeaway should be that you are consuming more food than most Third World countries.

**Have your fifteen minutes of fame.**
Knowing it will not be at the Oscars but rather on your front lawn, where you are engaged in some sort of drunken domestic dispute.

## Invent the cotton gin.
Been there, done that.

## Join the Flying Wallendas.
Even the Wallendas probably wish they had a different last name so they wouldn't have to fall hundreds of feet to their premature deaths.

## Make the "10 Most Wanted" list.
Your glee from being named best among your peers will instantly disappear when you realize you can't buy stamps or mail letters at the post office.

## Predict the future.
If you could really do this, I trust you'd be spending your time in a much more constructive way than you are right now.

## Reach a higher level of consciousness.
Put your quest for enlightenment on hold and just try not to lock yourself out of the house once a month or have to call the bank repeatedly because you forgot your ATM number.

### Ride a unicycle.
Ooh! Look at me, everyone! I'm riding a bicycle with only one tire!
Big whoop.

### Run a marathon.
A classic case of doing something just to prove to yourself and others
that you can do it regardless of how stupid it is. Choosing to undergo
pain for 26.2 miles should be considered grounds for undergoing a
CAT scan.

### See someone's aura.
If you truly have the ability to see someone's aura or field of energy,
why do you go out with such losers?

# Stupid Activities

You're always on the go, your social calendar is filled, and you don't have time to catch your breath. So why do you feel that you're spinning your wheels, spending your precious time doing trivial, meaningless things? Because you've got the cognitive skills of a paramecium and wouldn't recognize common sense if it was a neon sign on your forehead. To help you distinguish what is a worthwhile activity and what is a misguided, lame act of ignorance, here are some key acts of stupidity to try to avoid.

### Attend a poetry slam.
The only thing more depressing than writing bad poetry is listening to someone else's.

### Dance the macarena.
You looked stupid doing the macarena when it was briefly popular, and you'll look exponentially stupider now.

**Do performance art.**
Performance art is what artist wanna-bes do if they have no real talent. Stop thinking your body is an instrument of creativity and pick up a paintbrush for everyone's sake.

**Drum with the fellas.**
There is no warrior within you that will be released by drumming with a group of other men. There is only a rhythmically challenged turd.

**Enter a beauty contest.**
If pure evil exists in the world, you will find it either in senseless violence or a beauty contest. Pitting people who need copious amounts of external validation against one other is a cruel joke that should not be tolerated.

**Enter an animal-calling contest.**
After many years of practicing in the barn, you are ready to go public with your eerily realistic reproduction of the sound hogs make while they mate. You go, girl.

## Enter an eating contest.

Eating more than enough food in a less than enough amount of time is something your digestive system will want to question you about very soon.

## Go swing dancing.

Despite its popularity, swing dancing is basically an entire evening of spinning or being spun around. Dance if you absolutely must, but be aware that it is not much more than a socially approved form of getting dizzy.

## Go to a rave.

You apparently need a barrage of sensory stimuli to feel something. Ask yourself why you are so numb instead of staying up all night dancing to deafening music and consuming massive quantities of substances that make you talk fast.

## Go whaling.

While blubber remains a staple in the diet of some Eskimos, the whaling industry has remained significantly depressed for the last century or so. In any case, stay away from any field requiring you to kill something that is bigger than a three-bedroom colonial with a spear.

**Hang glide.**
You jump off a large mountain, relying purely on certain kinds of wind that may or may not arrive to keep you aloft. Am I missing something?

**Hunt.**
How and why does shooting Bambi with a high-powered rifle qualify as a sport? Fish, on the other hand, deserve to be caught because they have nothing better to do.

**Ice fish.**
Fishing through a foot of ice in below-freezing weather, however, indicates you have severe anger issues. Look deep within to find out why you need to express your dominance over creatures that can't talk and have no limbs.

**Join a secret society.**
The only secret, and it's not a very well-kept one, is that you and your buddies are a bunch of dweebs.

## Joust.

For the last half-millennium there have been precious few opportunities to knock opponents off a horse with a long pole except at Renaissance festivals and the occasional get-together in the Ozarks.

## Limbo.

Doing the limbo should be allowed only in the Caribbean after consuming many drinks with paper umbrellas. You deserve to slip a disk if limboing in any other circumstance.

## Logroll.

You're running on a piece of wood in a river, nothing more, nothing less.

## Paint your wagon.

First of all, it's curious and frankly a little disturbing that you own a wagon at your age. Second, why must you paint it?

## Participate in a line dance.

There are few sights more depressing than a group of adults doing a line dance. Boot-scoot yourself in the butt if you suddenly find yourself part of one.

## Play golf.

You spend five hours every chance you can to hit a white ball around, and your score has improved three strokes in ten years. Quality time this is not.

## Play the tambourine.

A donkey could play this instrument. So which member of the band are you sleeping with?

## Practice yoga or meditation.

Sorry, but bending, sitting, and thinking is not exercise or a therapeutic form of relaxation. If it is, I get a great stress-reducing workout just by taking a crap.

## Put another shrimp on the barbie.

Unless you're reading this Down Under, put another burger on the Weber like real Americans do.

## Rassle.

Rasslin' makes wrestling look noble.

**Read existential philosophy.**
You will first get a huge headache and then start questioning your very being.

**Ride a bicycle built for two.**
Something that looks like a lot of fun but is actually a big pain in the ass. Your partner is always peddling either too fast or too slow, and you'll just want to smack him.

**Roll out the barrels.**
Sure you'll probably be having a barrel of fun, but you're doing the polka, man!

**Scat.**
Ella Fitzgerald was the only person on earth who could do this without sounding like a total idiot.

**Send in the clowns.**
I can think of no situation that would be improved by sending in clowns. Besides, they're already here.

### Sing karaoke.
Singing is best left to professionals, not to people like you who make plants feel pain when you sing.

### Spend an inordinate amount of time working on your lawn.
Not only is having green grass far overrated while you're alive, it will matter even less when you're dead.

### Study the Cabala.
I am 99 44/100 percent sure that mystical Judaism is aeons beyond your comprehension. Start with those "Greatest Bible Stories" comic books and work your way up.

### Synchronize swim.
Do you really want to square dance in water? The requisite nose plugs alone should make you want to get immediately out of the pool.

### Yodel.
While certainly an interesting talent, yodeling is best left to Swiss men and women who seem to have lost something.

# 3

# Stupid Behavior

Are you frequently embarrassed? Do you often find yourself in sticky situations requiring legal intervention, bail money, or extreme levels of pity from those you've offended in some way? It is clear that you are behaving in stupid ways that are messing up your life. Get on the road less stupidly traveled by avoiding these kind of stupid behaviors.

## Attempt the Vulcan mind meld.
If you don't know what you're doing, this can lead to permanent melding.

## Dance with wolves.
This will not be some kind of mystical experience between man and nature but instead an exercise in Darwinian theory. You will, in other words, be torn to shreds.

**Duck and cover.**
Hiding under a desk during a nuclear attack would not have saved you in the 1950s, and it won't save you today.

**Eat anything with "Whiz" in its name.**
I don't care if it's 99 percent real cheese, it's still 1 percent "Whiz." You might also want to avoid food that is required to state that it is indeed "Food" on its package.

**Fold, spindle, or mutilate.**
Doing any of these can reportedly wreak havoc with the best-laid postal plans.

**Forget your partner's birthday.**
Do this once and the date will be permanently ingrained in your memory, years after you break up.

**Get a degree by mail.**
The University of Harvard, located in Bakersfield, California, and a frequent advertiser in *Easy Rider* magazine, should not be confused with Harvard University.

## Get court-martialed.

Military court makes the regular judicial system seem like a soiree. Don't break the rules of any organization that exists only to have rules.

## Give advice.

This will almost always just get you into trouble (present company excluded, of course). Focus on the plethora of stupid things you've done to mess up your own life.

## Heed advice.

So you're going to take the word of some know-it-all psychoquack just because he or she has a column and a radio show? Use your own common sense (assuming you have already purchased this book).

## Iron a shirt you're currently wearing.

Most people remove their shirts before ironing to prevent their skin from becoming a new form of synthetic fabric.

## Join a militia.

Living in a place that is wired to self-destruct if security is breached is by itself cause for alarm. Then there's the fact that you've declared war on a country that could wipe you and your wacky friends off the face of the earth with a World War II practice bomb.

## Keep eating after you're full.
This is nature's way to tell you that if you persist in eating you will eventually have to be taken out of your bedroom with a backhoe.

## Lead a coup.
Overthrowing a government is nice work if you can get it, but you will probably have to relocate.

## Live in an RV.
Your average recreation vehicle makes a studio apartment seem like Xanadu. While it's true that lab rats have more proportional living space, you will have a small refrigerator.

## Matchmake.
A rare opportunity to lose two friends in a single act of stupidity.

## Microwave your pet.
There is no situation in which this can turn out well.

## Mess with Texas.
Texans tell you not to do this, and I believe 'em.

## Pick up the feces of a lesser mammal for a living.
Walking dogs looks like fun but follows the standard 80/20 rule which states that 80 percent of everything in life is bad and 20 percent is good. In this case, we're talking 20 percent walking, 80 percent poop.

## Pretend you're interesting or funny if you're not.
This will only make it worse.

## Procrastinate.
Delaying the inevitable only makes that which you're reluctant to do more difficult. You should instead be eager for every opportunity to restore the damage you have done so far to your life.

## Pry into others' affairs.
Your affairs are probably far too bizarre to spend time and effort prying into anyone else's.

**Read the instructions on a shampoo bottle.**
If you still need to be reminded what to do with shampoo, you need more advice than that which comes with a health and beauty aid.

**Rotate your cuff.**
Since athletes always seem to be doing this and ruining their careers, I would advise rotating a different part of your body if you absolutely have to rotate.

**Seek sanctuary.**
I don't know what you did that you had to seek refuge from the law in a church, and I don't think I want to know.

**Spit in the wind.**
Or pull the mask of the old Lone Ranger. Or mess around with Jim.

**Stay on hold.**
Listening to Muzak while some minimum-wage teledrone decides to get back to you will make you hate the telephone and communication in general.

**Take crap from anyone.**
And you should because . . . ?

**Take some time off to discover yourself.**
After having lots of time to think about it, you will inevitably discover
that you like yourself a lot less than you did previously.

**Think locally, act globally.**
I think you're reading the bumper sticker wrong.

**Throw a keg party after the age of thirty.**
You will have three-quarters of a keg of beer in your bathtub for
weeks after your party. Recognize that, regrettably, you no longer have
the ability to drink gallons of beer in a single sitting.

**Throw caution to the wind.**
Throwing caution to the wind is very often the very last thing
someone says they will do before proceeding to lose all their money
and/or clothes.

## Wear camouflage.

This is a clear warning to others that one day you're going to think you're back in 'Nam and will have to defend the platoon at any and all costs. Keep your fatigues in the dresser unless you want people to move away from you slowly without making any sudden moves.

## Work on spec.

Giving away anything for free just makes people respect you even less, if that can be imagined.

# 4

# Stupid Beliefs

Do you repeatedly put your faith in people or institutions that inevitably let you down? Do you believe that people are out to get you? While it's possible that foreign agents have implanted a chip in your brain (which accounts for your occasional lapse into a Slovakian dialect), it's much more likely that you are believing things that have little basis in fact. Look over these prime examples of stupid beliefs to determine whether you are either trusting people too much or are running against the stream of what most of us have agreed is reality.

## Believe any government is out to get you.
Governments have better things to do than be concerned about the overwhelming insignificance of your existence.

## Believe armed forces commercials.
Your military career will not resemble that of a knight in shining armor but rather that of someone who has to run in the mud for long distances while carrying heavy objects.

**Believe in anarchy.**
The only reason you're around at all is that everyone who hates you knows they would go to jail if they whacked you. Consider yourself blessed for the social order that accounts for your very being.

**Believe in angels.**
It is comforting to think that there is a quasi-divine figure looking out for us, but there isn't. Quit this charade and deal with the fact that you are all alone in the world and will probably die a lonely death in a small, dark room in a rent-by-the-week boardinghouse.

**Believe in conspiracies or cover-ups.**
The only conspiracy that exists is that you have conspired to be a paranoid neurotic.

**Believe in fate.**
Believing there is some sort of grand design or that things happen for a reason only reinforces the idea that you do not control your own destiny. Walk in front of a bus and see what kismet has in store for you, fate boy.

**Believe in heroes.**
It is only a matter of time before your hero is revealed to be as
pathetic as you.

**Believe in miracle cures.**
You deserve to eat fish oil, oat bran, or beta-carotene if you believe in
miracle cures.

**Believe in miracles.**
Miracles only seem to have occurred centuries ago in places with a lot
of sand. Unless you are reading this in Mesopotamia, I would not wait
around for a sea to part or for someone to turn water into wine.

**Believe in original sin.**
You are not born with sin, but you certainly have had plenty of
opportunity to acquire lots of it along the way, haven't you?

**Believe in the devil.**
Evil does not reside within a red guy with horns. Evil resides within
the warped mind of someone who looks remarkably like you.

**Believe that teams are better than individuals.**
Teams naturally gravitate toward averageness and mediocrity, while individuals at least have a chance of greatness. Chances are, therefore, that you'd make a great team member.

**Believe you had a close encounter of the third kind.**
Aliens have better things to do than haul your sorry ass around the galaxy. If you were abducted, it was not by aliens but rather by some guys right out of *Deliverance*.

**Believe you should never quit something.**
Repeatedly attempting to succeed at something you consistently fail at is considerably stupider than failing at something once and moving on. Soar with your few strengths rather than plummet with your many weaknesses.

**Come up with your own theory of life.**
Unless your last name is Descartes or Hegel, don't bother me with this stuff.

**Expect the best-case scenario to occur.**
Never count on any situation to work out the best way it possibly can.

## Expect the worst-case scenario to occur.

Never count on any situation to work out the worst way it possibly can. If you haven't guessed it by now, life is basically one gradation of gray after another.

## Expect to be knighted.

Deal with the fact that the only Sir you can ever hope to be is Sir Wanker.

## Subscribe to any "ism."

"Isms" are meant for people who have no ideas of their own. I'd also not belong to any "ism" that would have you as a member.

## Think you are bipolar.

You're probably not bipolar as much as a total raving lunatic when you happen to skip that double latte with an extra shot of espresso and chocolate-chip scone you have most mornings.

## Think you are in "the movies" when you tear tickets.

You could be replaced by a machine with a relatively unsophisticated computer chip, although you did get to see *Titanic* thirty times.

# 5

# Stupid Communicating

How many of us can deny that we occasionally commit a faux pas or suddenly find ourselves in a conversation revolving around the barometer and/or dew point? If you regularly have difficulty conveying your thoughts or connecting with others, however, there's a good chance you are a stupid communicator. Check out these examples of stupid communication before you seriously consider becoming a mime.

### Argue with a religious fanatic.
Even if you are right, which of course you will be, you are being stupid if you think you can win this kind of argument. Keep moving or be prepared for a conversation with no purpose or conclusion.

### Ask a woman if she's pregnant.
There's about a fifty-fifty chance that she's not pregnant at all but has simply discovered the miracle that is Krispy Kreme doughnuts. Do not find out this information firsthand.

## Ask someone what their sign is.

Don't get out much, do you? Put your Nehru suit, Earth Shoes, and collection of 8-tracks into storage and try not to make it so obvious that you are a living, breathing anachronism.

## Be politically correct.

If I hear the words *disenfranchised, enabled*, or *empowered* one more time, I'm going to give you a very politically incorrect smack in your marginalized kisser.

## Call a woman a "gal," "the wife," or "my better half."

Apparently you were watching wrestling or maybe taking out the trash during the women's liberation movement. In a nutshell, women won the right to be independent from troglodytes such as yourself.

## Call your wife or husband, even in jest, "Mommy" or "Daddy."

I get chills just thinking about this. Avoid these terms of endearment or deal with consequences of Oedipal proportions.

## Cotton for something.
You are among a small number of people who use "cotton" as a verb. Please help make this number even smaller.

## Debate the relative quality of old sitcoms.
Finding yourself in a heated discussion of the comparative value of *Green Acres* versus *Petticoat Junction* will just make you hate yourself even more.

## Discuss confidential information on a cell phone.
Blackmailers and/or the feds will be on you like white on rice. Do all your insider trading and other white collar crimes the sensible way, i.e., face-to-face.

## Eulogize someone as a "dork," "dink," or "doorknob."
Of course the guy was all of these, but there's no need to bring it up at his funeral, for heaven's sake. Do the right thing and tell him he is all these things while he's still alive.

**Footnote your conversations.**
You have apparently been in grad school much too long. Try to
remember that citing sources for all your ideas is not required in the
real world.

**Invent your own language.**
This shows real gumption on your part but also a fair share of
stupidity given that you will be able to communicate with no one.

**Pass on urban legends or myths.**
It is sad how some people feel the need to spread sensational stories
that have no basis in fact simply because they have nothing else to
say. Resist the temptation to repeat these tales, especially the one
about Richard Gere and his interest in rodents.

**Refer to yourself by a single name.**
Cher, Madonna, and Sting can get away with this because they have
talent. Unless you're going to call yourself "Goofy," you better use
both your names.

**Send an annual letter to your friends and family.**
No one cares that you and your family went to Six Flags in May or
that Bobby scored a goal at soccer camp. Just because you have to

endure your mundane existence does not mean that the rest of us should.

## Speak in iambic pentameter.

Speaking in any poetic form will make everyone you meet want to put you and the nearest heavy object into direct, immediate contact.

## Speak in tongues.

You and reality are no longer in close proximity when you start speaking languages that no longer or never existed. Come back from thirteenth-century Gaeldom or that planet in our neighboring galaxy before you freak everyone the hell out.

## Use the words *bunghole, dillweed,* or *jugs* in an interview.

Human resource experts recommend using more action-oriented terms such as *pinhead, skank,* and *hooters*.

## Write in hieroglyphics.

People will get tired of trying to decipher your messages, especially if they're mostly about hunting animals with sticks.

# 6

# Stupid Crimes

Do you often find plain, unmarked vehicles following your car? Do you frequently hear a clicking on your phone and find strange electronic devices in your houseplants? Has there been a laundry truck with a satellite dish on its roof parked outside your house for more than three months? Are there a couple of large, swarthy men standing on your sidewalk right now? If you answered yes to any of these questions, you may be in trouble with the law. Committing crimes is your way to bring attention to yourself and tell the world that you're not the human sagebrush you were growing up. Here are some more popular stupid crimes to avoid lest you find yourself the girlfriend of an ex-welterweight champion of the world.

## Abscond.
It doesn't matter at all where you've absconded. The mere fact that you've absconded means you need a very good lawyer.

## Be put on double secret probation.

You're probably going to get kicked out of college anyway at this point so you might as well throw a toga party.

## Bribe a cop.

We've all been tempted to slip a cop a twenty when he asks to see a driver's license and registration. This at best will lead to an embarrassing situation and at worst to something not unlike the Rodney King video.

## Commit random acts of violence.

Random acts of kindness will be received far more enthusiastically.

## Confess.

Admitting guilt will only get you into more trouble than you are already in. There are plenty of reasons to account for the presence of that naked person in your bed once you really stop to consider the total range of possible explanations.

## Engage in a cover-up.

Covering up a crime is almost always worse than the original crime. And if you were dumb enough to commit a crime that you now have to cover up, why do you expect the cover-up to go smoothly?

**Fudge your résumé.**

Your employers will eventually discover that you did not really graduate summa cum laude, earn a masters degree, and most important, serve as CEO of General Motors from 1981 to 1986.

**Go AWOL.**

You are trying to hide from people who kill other people for a living and own bombs that can make ninety-degree turns. I think they'll be able to find you hanging out at your girlfriend's place watching soaps.

**Incite a riot.**

Don't go stirring up trouble by turning a crowd of peaceful protestors into an angry mob. Use your outstanding charisma for more personally rewarding purposes, like persuading old people to give you their life savings.

**Issue your own form of currency.**

Most if not all other people in the known universe will not recognize the monetary unit you have developed for your own personal use. Please use the form of currency the rest of us have agreed is money.

## Jump ball.

You must have seen *The Fugitive* by now and realize that life spent on the lam is no life at all.

## Keep evidence.

Many criminologists will tell you that people keep evidence of a crime because they want to get caught. A little tip: The key thing about being a successful criminal is not to get caught.

## Lie under oath.

You've sworn on the Bible in a court of law to tell the truth, the whole truth, and nothing but the truth. If this isn't enough impetus to tell the truth, you deserve to go to jail.

## Loan-shark.

There is nothing morally wrong with charging usurious interest rates to people who cannot obtain a loan in the traditional manner, but the need to break thumbs or kneecaps once in a while will start to get on your nerves.

## Remove the warning label from a pillow or mattress.

A victimless crime, yes, but one more chink in the armor that holds society together.

## Resist arrest.

Although you may be perfectly innocent, duking it out with one or more armed beefcakes in blue will only lead to more problems. View any entanglements with the law as an opportunity to see how the legal system works and then be sued for millions of dollars.

## Rob from the poor and give to the rich.

Besides being perceived as a lot less socially redeeming, robbing from the poor and giving to the rich will net you a lot less money than the traditional idea of robbing from the rich and giving to the poor.

## Scam an insurance company.

After these people get through with you, you will wish the accident or death you faked was real.

## Smuggle in dope from a foreign country.

Go out and rent *Midnight Express* this minute if you are still considering this.

## Steal cable.

One day they will track down where that extra signal of HBO is going and ban you permanently from getting cable. If you thought television sucked when you got fifty-eight channels, wait until you get just five.

## Steal toilet paper.

This is pitiful even for you. In some countries, you know, carrying a concealed roll of commercial-strength toilet paper will fetch three years in a squalid jail cell.

## Violate your parole.

The system was dumb enough to let you out, but by violating your parole you'll prove even dumber by making them take you back.

# 7

# Stupid Decisions

As I discussed extensively in my last book, *What the Hell Were You Thinking?* and plan to discuss even more about in my next book, *Foolish Choices, Stupid People*, we are all capable of making stupid decisions now and then. Still, that is no excuse for the amazing number and variety of errors in judgment you seem to make on a regular basis. Gain some very needed wisdom by trying not to make some of these stupid decisions.

**Abdicate the throne.**
You're going to give up a life of pomp, circumstance, and totally undeserved perks for some commoner? Don't be stupid and mess up your life. It's good to be king!

**Donate your organs while you are still alive.**
A generous gesture but most doctors recommend you hold off doing this until you are dead.

**Drop out of school.**

An education is the smartest investment anyone can make, which is why a dunce like you is dropping out. Go back to school before you find yourself doing the graveyard shift in a tollbooth on the New Jersey Turnpike.

**Eat Mentos.**

This will tell the Mentos people that their commercials are working. And we don't want to encourage that, do we?

**Enter animal husbandry.**

Becoming a husband to any animal besides a human is something you gals should really think twice about.

**Fire a middle-aged, African-American, handicapped woman.**

Save time by just issuing a blank check to her lawyers and setting up a time for *60 Minutes* to visit.

**Follow the yellow brick road.**

Sound advice if you want a witch from hell and about a thousand winged monkeys chasing you and your buddies clear across Oz. That's what you get for listening to a bunch of out-of-control, sex-crazed munchkins.

## Get cloned.
There's one too many of you already.

## Go on a hunger strike.
You will lose one-third of your body weight, and people will still be treating marmots unfairly or whatever the hell your stupid beef is. Protest by a means that does not involve personal starvation.

## Have your head frozen when you're dead.
Even if they do discover a cure for whatever killed you, do you really want to be woken up a hundred years from now with just a recently thawed head?

## Hire a baby-sitter named Vixen, Supervixen, or Ultravixen.
While your baby-sitter could just be named after some very popular film stars of the 1970s, chances are she's not a very good role model for your child.

## Join a committee.
Committees consist of people who think they are doing something important when all they are really doing is serving on committees.

## Learn your genetic profile.
Do you really want to know that you are predisposed to a fatal disease? I'd rather continue worrying about things like the low batteries in my remote control.

## Live anyplace in which "good weather" is the primary selling point.
There is a direct correlation between good weather and bad karma. Just take a look at a map and you'll see exactly what I mean.

## Marry a mail-order bride.
They certainly look great when you order them, but so do those hip waders in the L. L. Bean catalog until you get 'em on and you realize they're not nearly as comfortable as you thought they'd be.

## Move back home.
I don't care how much money you're going to save, you will regret it immediately after your mom declares every Tuesday "Wash Your Hair Day."

**Move in with your in-laws.**
Much like moving back home but worse because at least you already know how weird your own parents are.

**Name your baby O. J.**
The kid will have a happier life if you name him Adolph, Benito, or Putz.

**Own a pit-bull terrier.**
If you still own or are thinking of getting this breed of dog after knowing their penchant for going berserk, you need to begin electroshock therapy immediately.

**Put your child on the fast track.**
The earlier you start your child on the path of success, the earlier he or she will begin to develop issues that allow people like me to make a very nice dollar.

**Respond to an ad for "models."**
This will not be your big break. This will be your big opportunity to get naked before a complete stranger with a camera.

**Round up the usual suspects.**
A common technique in law enforcement but a less than scientific way to get your man. Try looking for evidence first, then rounding up some likely suspects.

**Secede from the Union.**
The Union gets very mad when anyone decides to create their own country with its own laws, especially if it's about the right to own other people.

**Send away for anything you saw on the inside of a matchbook.**
Congratulations! You just spent $49.95 to find out that, yes, you can draw the little pony.

**Take a sabbatical.**
A great idea, but when you return to work no one will remember your name or what you do exactly.

**Take any form of public transportation in which livestock is permitted aboard.**
This is a sign, at the very least, that the vehicle probably receives less than regular safety inspections.

**Volunteer for a medical research study.**
You must be pretty desperate to be a paid guinea pig for an experimental drug or procedure. Try earning money in a manner in which growing another limb is not a possibility.

**Wait to retire to have fun.**
You'll be old and tired and not remember exactly what fun is except you think it might have had something to do with not working as much.

**Wear a ponytail if you are not a little girl.**
Ponytails on adult men are a desperate attempt to hang on to whatever little youth and/or hair they have left.

# 8

# Stupid Entertainment

In our society where entertainment rules, how you choose to spend your free time reveals key insights into your personality and emotional health. What might appear to be on the surface a simple act of stupidity—say, spending good money to see a performance by Gallagher—is often a desperate plea for help or possibly a warning sign of an impending stroke or cerebral hemorrhage. As life in America continues to be a series of Disneyesque experiences, beware of these sorts of stupid entertainment options.

## Appreciate Yanni.
You are mistaking plaintive wailing for music. Laboratory rats forced to listen to both Yanni and John Tesh have either eaten their cage mates or experienced significant brain shrinkage.

## Attend a cockfight.
Watching two chickens fight to the death is not what I call entertainment. Choose something more wholesome, like dwarf-tossing.

**Break into vaudeville.**
I admire your fortitude and your well-honed comedic timing, but the vaudeville circuit is now limited to the clubhouse of the Sun City retirement community.

**Do the Village People's "Y.M.C.A." thing.**
This was marginally unstupid for about a week in 1979. After that it was and is synonymous with stupidity.

**Do the wave.**
The wave was something baseball fans invented when they realized how incredibly boring the game really was. Unfortunately, doing the wave is now even more boring than watching baseball.

**Enjoy mimes.**
Although I may be wrong on this, I do believe the law now allows ordinary citizens to kill mimes on sight.

**Get addicted to a soap opera.**
Soon you will be taping episodes of *The Days of Our Lives* and watching them at night. Then your life will officially be over.

**Go to a comedy club.**
Comedy clubs contain less comedy per square inch than all other places I can think of, except perhaps group therapy sessions and feminist rallies.

**Go to a dubbed movie.**
Hearing someone speak French while hearing someone else speak bad English is bad for your brain.

**Go to a strip club.**
So you need to be hornier? I don't think so. Furthermore, having to pay someone to sit on your lap is only admitting to yourself and others that no one will do it because they really want to.

**Go to any Andrew Lloyd Webber show.**
There is no story, and you can't hum the music one second after it stops.

**Go to any movie starring a current or past member of *Saturday Night Live*.**
Throw your nine dollars down the drain and save yourself two hours of valuable time.

## Go to any performance "on ice."

Actors on skates are not a pretty sight. Expect something called "Grease on Ice" to be just like it sounds.

## Listen to an oldies station.

Paul Revere and the Raiders were not worth listening to in 1966, much less today. Join the rest of the world in what we call "the present."

## Listen to golf on the radio.

This takes way more imagination than the average human being is capable of and will really mess with your mind.

## Sit in the front row of a comedy show.

You're just asking to have your appearance, occupation, geographic origin, or close family relative turned into comedic fodder. Skip this one, however, if you happen to be either an exhibitionist or a masochist.

## Wait for Beta to come back.

Just admit you were wrong and everyone else in the world, including most SONY executives, were right.

**Watch Infomercials.**
Watching someone shred lettuce or chop bok choy is like watching paint dry. I don't care how many different ways the amazing gadget can do it.

**Watch the Classic Sports Network.**
It didn't matter at all who won the U.S. Open in 1971 and it somehow matters even less now.

**Watch the Weather Channel.**
Reexamine your priorities if you enjoy learning the three-day forecast for Pakistan.

# 9

# Stupid Experiences

Are you one of those people who will try anything once? There's a fair chance that that which you are trying for the first time will turn out to be an unpleasant experience or possibly even require employment of the jaws of life. Here are some types of stupid experiences that should not be tried at home or anywhere else for that matter.

## Appear on a daytime talk show.
Your need to reveal your pathetic lifestyle on national television is simultaneously stupid and pitiable. Keep the fact that you're a 400-pound transgender Goth to yourself.

## Become a cast member of MTV's *The Real World.*
You will have every minute of your life taped, with the worst moments broadcast around the world.

## Become a minstrel.
Performing in blackface today is as entertaining as ever, but you may have trouble getting gigs.

## Drink mead or grog.
The Middle Ages ended some five hundred years ago. Put down your goblet and try to keep up with the rest of us in the Information Age.

## Eat mutton.
You do realize that mutton is sheep, don't you?

## Go to junior high school.
I know this probably can't be avoided if you're an adolescent, but I thought I'd mention it anyway. The good thing is that life can't get too much worse than your typical junior high school experience.

## Go to spring break after you've graduated.
You'll suddenly realize your youth is over when you begin to question the wisdom of jumping from one hotel-room balcony to another.

## Go to your high school prom.
You survived both junior high and high school. Don't press your luck.

## Grade papers.
Your gung-ho attitude to help students learn will rapidly fade after spending your weekends reading three hundred blue books, many of them starting off, "This question is a very good question and a question that is worth answering with a good answer."

## Have an out-of-body experience.
You will regret looking down at yourself from the ceiling, trust me. Bring your spirit back into your body as soon as you feel it getting antsy.

## Hear voices in your head.
A disturbing development even if you're not really picking up messages from extraterrestrials or foreign operatives. Have this checked out, especially if you're being told to "Come to the light."

## Join a posse.
Let the pros chase down those fellas who robbed the local bank.

## Jump into a mosh pit.
Throwing yourself headfirst into a teeming pit of testosterone will seem fun until the crowd gets bored of passing you and drops you on your head.

## Live in a parallel universe.
I would stick with this universe, but that's just my advice.

## Pull on someone's finger upon demand.
If you've never done this, you will be disappointed with what happens next.

## Purge your digestive system.
Removing the contents of your digestive system before full processing almost always does more harm than good. I would trust nature to tell you when the food in your body no longer belongs there.

## Run with the bulls.
Running with the bulls serves a vital purpose in a society in which men are judged by their machismo. You, however, are not a brave Spaniard but an American numbskull.

## See your parents having sex.
This will set you back years in your sexual development, if not turn you into a eunuch right on the spot. Pretend they were just playing naked Twister.

**Spontaneously combust.**
Although rare, spontaneous combustion is damaging to those who
undergo it, as well as to those who happen to be in the general area
when it occurs. Look for the classic warning signs, i.e., sparks or
heavy blue smoke emanating from the head.

**Tip a cow.**
This is admittedly very funny but serves no socially redeeming
function.

**Tip an outhouse.**
Now this is extremely funny and serves many socially redeeming
functions.

**Visit a meat-packing plant.**
Knowing how a hot dog is made will not make you want to eat one.
In fact, there's a good chance you will become a vegan and militant
member of PETA.

**Wake up in a foreign country.**
You've fallen asleep at the airport, and the next thing you know
you're in Zaire or Singapore. Yes, a rare occurrence, but definitely an
annoying and puzzling one.

# 10

# Stupid Fantasies

Reality check! You must stop living in the fantasy world you have constructed as a protective mechanism and reenter the real world with all its imperfections. Your pattern of denial and history of delusional behavior only reinforces your penchant to flee versus facing your many demons. Here is a set of ill-advised fantasies that very well may resemble your own personal portfolio of stupid ones.

## Assume you are God.
Thinking you are God is a clear sign that you have what we psychiatrists call "delusions of grandeur." This is the case if, for example, you list "Messiah" on the occupation line of your 1040 tax form.

## Be a geisha.
Four years of college and you dream of spending your life giving men baths? Reexamine your career goals.

## Become a gondolier.

The waiting list to become a gondolier in Venice is decades long and considerably longer if you live anywhere between Altoona, Pennsylvania, and Winnemucca, Nevada.

## Believe you are a vampire or witch.

You have no special powers except an extraordinary ability to annoy people.

## Build your dream house.

Your dream house will become your worst nightmare somewhere between the discovery of the underground stream and the installation of the wrong foam insulation.

## Claim you're a virgin.

Yeah, and I'm not a highly trained psychotherapist with his own radio show and syndicated column.

## Date a mermaid.

A powerful fantasy, yes, but her love of chum will eventually prove to be a huge turnoff.

**Date a model.**
They are tall and gorgeous, and you will have nothing to say to them.
Date someone who does not receive money to stare blankly.

**Dream that soccer will be the next big American sport.**
They've been predicting this since before they said we'd convert to the
metric system. No one in his or her right mind will or should like a
sport in which a 0–0 score occurs with regular frequency.

**Expect a real estate transaction to go smoothly.**
Both buying and selling a house are inherently fraught with things that
will go awry. Consider any real estate transaction that takes place at
all to be a minor miracle and you should be okay.

**Fantasize that you'll have a good New Year's Eve.**
You'll go out for dinner, have a few drinks, go to bed, and try to stay
up until midnight to watch the ball drop on TV like every other New
Year's since you turned thirty.

**Have a past-life experience.**
There is no fourteenth-century medieval princess or seventeenth-century feudal lord inside you informing your present consciousness. There is only a very-early-twenty-first-century moron.

**Have someone do your laundry or clean your house.**
You will lose your sense of reality when you lose touch with the ordinary drudgery of everyday life. Don't reinforce your remarkable penchant for sloth.

**Imagine that you are communicating with your cat.**
Your cat is not nodding knowingly when you ask him a question. He is shaking his head because he can't believe what a cluck he has for an owner.

**Join the Foreign Legion.**
Just finding the Foreign Legion at this point seems beyond the realm of possibility.

**Pretend you're two sizes smaller than you really are.**
You're now telling the world that you're not only fat but that you're in the much more pitiful state of fat denial.

**Recall a traumatic childhood experience while in therapy.**
No, you did not fall through the ice on the skating pond and almost die when you were eight, like your therapist would like to have you believe. Your sister threw a snowball in your ear just like you remembered.

**Think you and your "companion animal" are soul mates.**
You are not equal partners with your dog unless you too lick your balls and eat cigarette butts.

**Train to be a boxer.**
Exchanging punches to the body and head is certainly an exciting way of life but rarely allows you to advance much further than Stage 1 or 2 of Maslow's hierarchy.

**Wait for Mr. or Ms. Right.**
There is no such person, and you will be a bitter, shriveled-up virgin by the time you realize it. Settle like the rest of us for Mr. or Ms. Kinda Right.

# Stupid Feelings

All of us are naturally wired to feel a wide range of emotions such as anger, resentment, jealousy, and hate. If these sort of feelings are getting in the way of more positive ones, however, you are allowing your emotions to control you rather than the other way around. At least this is what your run-of-the-mill psychiatrist would have you believe. I would just say that you've got a pack of stupid feelings, nothing more and nothing less, and point out others just like these so you know 'em when you see 'em.

## Accentuate the positive.

Always looking on the bright side accounts for your phenomenal inability to grasp the obvious. Rather than accentuate the positive or eliminate the negative, I'd recommend messing around with Mr. In-Between.

## Blame others.
Realizing you are in control of your own destiny is the first step toward achieving the maturity and wisdom that has eluded you for so long. You have only yourself to blame for, say, throwing up on your driving instructor.

## Care what people say or think of you.
It just doesn't matter, someone very wise once said.

## Carry emotional baggage.
It's time you get over the nightmare that was your junior high school production of *Auntie Mame*. Loss of urinary tract control can happen to anyone in periods of high stress, medical research has shown.

## Don't worry, be happy.
The few people in the world who feel they have nothing to worry about pose the greatest threat to the rest of us who know there is plenty to worry about.

## Envy others.
If I can offer any comfort, you should know that everyone you envy is just as insecure, fatuous, and hopeless as you. That's what I'm here for.

**Feel guilt.**
You should not feel guilty about all those bad things you do on a regular basis. You should feel pure, unadulterated shame.

**Feel like a victim.**
I sympathize with your having been forced to take shop class in high school, but it is time to let go of the tragedies of the past.

**Feel like you have no purpose in life.**
This is not true at all. Working at Jack-in-the-Box serves a vital role in today's fast-paced society.

**Feel like you know it all.**
Not only do you not know it all, you barely know how to spell *all*.

**Feel too passionate about anything that can break, be stolen, or wear out.**
This is why you still mourn the demise of your troll doll that your sister melted in her EasyBake oven.

**Get emotionally involved with a sports team.**
It's inevitable that your home team will eventually pack up all its stuff and move in the middle of the night for a better deal (kinda like your girlfriend did.)

**Get inspired by motivational sayings.**
Or, for that matter, get motivated by inspirational sayings.

**Hate men just because they are men.**
Yes, we are dogs with car keys when you get right down to it, but it's not our fault.

**Have regrets.**
There is nothing you can do about the missed opportunities of your past. Redirect your energy toward trying to minimize the inevitable missed opportunities of your future.

**Love your enemies.**
I don't know who came up with this crazy idea, but I do know that I hate him.

**Obsess about low self-esteem.**
Chances are you already think you're smarter and cuter than you really are.

**Refuse to admit you were wrong.**
If this is the case, you must hardly speak. Fess up whenever you screw up even if it does require your having an "It was my fault" rubber stamp made.

**Think you are totally stressed out.**
You're stressed out because you forgot to set your VCR to record "Must See TV"? Real stress occurred sometime between the Black Death and the Spanish Inquisition.

**Weep uncontrollably.**
Regularly sobbing for no particular reason is cause for alarm, even if we are talking about the remarkable sadness that is your life.

**Whine about not getting into the college or university of your choice.**
You're forty years old. It's time to move on to whining about more important things.

# 12

# Stupid Finance

Do you and money tend to go separate ways? While it could just be bad luck (how were you to know that your financial advisor would take off for Bali with all your savings and that hottie for a secretary?), it may be that you have bad business sense or are fiscally irresponsible. Get your financial life in order by not falling for any of these stupid financial blunders.

## Bounce a check.

Having your name posted on the wall of a restaurant where you bounced a check is the modern day equivalent of being placed in the stocks in the village square. You do not need to invite more shame into your psychological house.

## Bury money in your yard.

You apparently lived through the Depression or have an unnatural mistrust of banks. There is nothing inherently wrong with this except you will soon get old, mistake your money for cabbage, and eat it.

**Buy high, sell low.**
Like many if not most things in your life, this is exactly opposite of the approach you should be taking.

**Buy things you cannot pay for.**
You don't have to be Adam Smith to understand the most basic law of economics, but let me break it down for you: If the thing you want to purchase exceeds the amount of money you own, you should not buy it. Does that help at all?

**Fly a discount airline.**
You should not scrimp on certain things, one of those being things that transport your body at speeds of five hundred miles per hour to heights of 37,000 feet.

**Get audited.**
Once these bastards get a grip on your financial balls they never let go. Fork out the dough up front before they come knocking at your door.

**Give money to any organization with "Liberation" or "Freedom Fighters" in its name.**
You will soon have an FBI file bigger than Sinatra's.

## Go to the "early dinner" in Florida to save a couple of bucks.

The human stomach was simply not designed to eat dinner at 4:30. Splurge and eat dinner at six or seven o'clock like people in the rest of the world do.

## Go to Vegas to win money.

You go to Vegas to eat cheap food, drink cheap drinks, see scantily clad women, hear cheesy singers, and lose one hundred dollars gambling.

## Lend or borrow money to or from a friend.

Shakespeare was dead right on this one. That "All the world's a stage" stuff I'm not so sure about.

## Marry for money.

There is, unfortunately, a directly inverse relationship between the amount of money a potential spouse has and how happy you will be. This is one of those checks and balances of nature that keeps the species perpetuating.

## Mistake credit for debt.

A credit card is your way to get thirty days of free credit, not a way to pay 18 percent interest compounded annually until you've paid about a thousand dollars for a lousy sweater and three pairs of socks.

## Owe money to anyone named Big Daddy.

There are valid reasons he has earned this nickname, and you don't want to learn them.

## Pay retail.

Paying full price for anything is not only foolish but an insult to whoever is selling you the item. Haggle even if you are Midwestern.

## Pick up a penny because it's lucky.

Finding a penny isn't lucky unless you consider picking up a dirty, germ-infested, essentially valueless piece of metal off the street a positive step in your life.

## Play the lottery.

You have a better chance of getting hit by a satellite or even getting your lame poems published than winning the lottery. Don't give any more money to the government than you already have to.

**Play three-card monty.**
You have better odds playing the lottery.

**Put up collateral.**
You're in way over your head once you start putting up your personal belongings as collateral for a loan. Do so and start getting comfortable with the idea of mass transit and staying at the "Y."

**Rent.**
Renting is for people who can't beg, borrow, or steal a few thousand bucks as down payment on a house or else don't plan on being in one place too long. Being either poor or transient is no way to go though life, sweetie.

**Save coupons.**
You've exchanged thirty minutes of your life to save twenty cents off three gallons of Clamato juice. Reexamine your priorities.

# 13

# Stupid Goals

Setting goals and trying to reach them is an essential part of staying excited about life. Many people, however, set their sights too short or establish misguided personal and professional objectives. Committing to be a far more evil person, for example, is a goal probably not worth pursuing for a number of reasons. Here are some other stupid goals to resist striving for when you think about what you want to do with the rest of your life.

### Aspire to be a ninja.
There is hardly any call for ninjas these days, at least in these parts. Have you considered career opportunities within the samurai arena?

### Be someone you're not.
This is sound advice unless of course the person you're being is far superior to the person you really are. Hmm, maybe you should forget this one.

**Become a clown.**
You're already a clown if you are thinking of becoming a professional one. Another thing you should know: Clowns don't make people happy but rather scare the living bejesus out of them.

**Become a contortionist.**
Just because you have the rare ability to bend backward and stick your head between your legs does not mean you should turn it into a career.

**Become a dancer.**
Unless you're talking ballet, "dancing" means taking your clothes off for men in cheap suits.

**Become a farmer.**
Farming is indeed a noble profession but a stupid one unless you're already rich. Grow tomatoes in your backyard like the rest of us.

**Become a forest ranger.**
Sitting in a tower for months at a time in the remote wilderness with no human contact will put a damper on your social life. Find a job where there is more than one person per 100,000 square acres of land.

## Become a pirate.
Taking to the open seas to loot and plunder is not only unethical but rarely offers major medical, much less dental insurance.

## Become a rodeo clown.
Rodeo clowns are even less funny than regular clowns, and they are often trampled to death while trying to avoid bucking broncos with sore testicles.

## Become a spy.
With the Cold War over, the only secret worth selling to the Russians these days would be the formula for Coke or McDonald's special sauce.

## Conform.
Do you really want to conform to the norms of a society whose greatest contributions are recognized around the world as *Baywatch* and monster-truck rallies?

## Discover the meaning of life.
It is fruitless to search for the meaning of life, and even if you did happen to stumble upon it, you would be disappointed to learn that it is mostly about stuff that is readily available for purchase at any mall.

**Go to Hollywood to become a star.**
Ninety percent of the lucky people who go to Hollywood to become
famous actors become food service personnel. Ninety percent of the
unlucky people who go to Hollywood to become famous actors
become sex-trade personnel.

**Plan great things for the new millennium.**
The new millennium will be just like the old millennium except that
we'll all write down the wrong century on our checks for a while.

**Read people's minds.**
You can't figure out how to make long-grain rice or fix a leaky faucet
and you're attempting to read other people's minds? Try to read more
than a small portion of your own mind before trying to read others'.

**Save the world.**
Set your sights on a somewhat more achievable goal, such as getting
through Letterman without falling asleep or remembering to wear
underwear.

**Understand the tax implications of capital gains, the
Roth I.R.A., or long-term annuities.**
Just the concept of compound interest boggles the mind.

## Want to be normal.

Normalcy is one of the most sought after traits that no one wants if they have it. Fortunately, it is something that you have extremely little chance of being anyway.

# 14

# Stupid Habits

Have you been told you get on people's nerves? Do people flee when they see you coming? Are you obnoxious to the point where your sheer existence causes pain to everyone with whom you have contact? If so, it is readily apparent that you are an individual with uncommonly stupid habits. It is time you rid yourself of these practices before you cause more harm to others and yourself. Review these seminal stupid habits to see if they sound a little too familiar.

## Buy supersize food.
Regularly upgrading to a "Biggie" fries or sixty-four-ounce pop for an extra quarter at fast-food restaurants is the reason you're often told that you resemble the Michelin Man when you're naked.

## Cross each day off the calendar.
Why do you take satisfaction in celebrating the passage of time that brings you closer and closer to your own death? Life is not something

to measure but rather something to face with normal dread and despair.

### Eavesdrop.
You really don't want to know what Joe Bag-of-Donuts is thinking, do you? I didn't think so.

### Floss in public.
I shudder just thinking about this.

### Go through people's medicine cabinets.
Are you happy you now know that your friend has a chronic yeast infection and that your boss chafes in areas you never wanted to envision?

### Interpret your dreams.
Dreams are not windows into your soul but rather weird stuff you were thinking about just before you fell asleep. Why you were thinking about doing your grade school principal I have no idea.

## Let out a primal scream.

Shouting will have little effect on venting your own anger, but it will make other people as angry as you, which, I guess, is some compensation.

## Live in the future.

Living in a time that is even slightly ahead of the rest of us will be less cool than you think it will be. Yes, you will know who wins horse races and stuff, but you will also know that you will stub your toe and you won't be able to do anything about it.

## Make quotation marks with your fingers when you talk.

This is an annoying habit that will just make people hate you more than they already do.

## Read your horoscope.

So you're going to fall deeply in love today because a giant rock a million miles away moved slightly to the right? Get your head out of Uranus!

## Refuse to change with the times.

Those who are most able to adjust to change are almost always happier and more successful than those who are less able. This means you should probably stop wearing britches and referring to everyone as "Ye."

## Sing "We Are the Champions" or any other song by Queen.

This is just one of those rules of life that you just don't question.

## Smoke cigars.

They are a silly, phallic prop that smell bad and taste worse. Hence their popularity.

## Use an organizer or planner.

You are carrying around a five pound To Do list that set you back around fifty bucks.

## Use fabric softener.

Fabric softener is the biggest scam going since medicine tonic. Beyond that, why are you following the advice of a fictitious, obnoxious little bear who tells you to put chemicals on your clothes to make them soft?

# 15

# Stupid Hobbies

What you choose to do in your free time is your business, but if it is truly stupid, it becomes Dr. Larry's business. Your participation in stupid arts and crafts, stupid recreational activities, and stupid organizations is giving people the impression that you must be a stupid person, a not unfair assessment of the situation. Quit these types of stupid hobbies ASAP before you find yourself at a Dickens Village convention in Des Moines.

## Act out Civil War battles.
Quit spending every weekend waging mock battles as a Confederate or Union soldier and come join the rest of us in reality, will you? And get rid of that musket before you hurt someone.

## Be a team mascot.
Just because you couldn't make the team doesn't mean you should wear a forty-pound bear suit all year to be near athletes.

## Brew your own beer.

If you've ever smelled beer brewing, you should already know that you don't want to have barrels of hops, yeast, malt, and barley fermenting in your house. Go buy a six-pack when you want a beer, like people who aren't insane.

## Do jigsaw puzzles.

Jigsaw puzzles require no skills at all except a rare ability to withstand inordinate quantities of boredom in a single sitting.

## Get involved with puppets.

Anthropomorphic figures made of fabric which fit on your hand are obviously evil. This also applies, by the way, to sock monkeys.

## Keep a diary or journal.

Living the minutia that is your life is something you have no choice about. Documenting it is just perverse.

## Keep bees.

They will eventually all escape and sting you until you resemble the Stay-Puff Marshmallow Man. And oh yes: The last time I looked, I believe there were many hobbies that do not involve insects and poisonous venom.

### Knit, do needlepoint, or cross-stitch.
You have taken three months out of your life to make something it would take a machine thirty seconds. Give yourself an extra kick in the butt if you own a loom.

### Own a horse.
Why anyone would want to constantly feed and groom a half-ton, methane-producing, dumb-as-a-box-of-hammers animal is beyond me. Rent one when you feel the need to sit on one.

### Perform any form of magic.
Magic is the only socially acceptable form of fraud I can think of (at least professional wrestling doesn't even pretend to be real). Talk to me when you really can make an elephant disappear.

### Raise emu.
Emu are just the latest in a long line of animals to be pronounced the next major source of food when in fact no one who has any choice in the matter will ever want to eat one.

## Whittle.

The ability to make a small stick out of a large stick is not something you should show off.

## Write haiku.

Unrhymed, seventeen-syllable poetry makes ordinary, grating poetry seem appealing.

# 16

# Stupid Ideas

Dr. Larry can't help you raise your IQ, but he can detect a stupid idea a mile away. Stupid ideas may seem harmless but in fact can cause long-term damage to your life or create a ripple effect of stupidity that ends up seeping into every nook and cranny of your being. Here's a wide variety of stupid ideas that you should not ignore, as that would be yet another one of your stupid ideas.

### Bring your dog to work.
Dogs do not understand the human concept of work and exposing one to it will make him or her worry whether the dog in the next office is getting more food than he or she is.

### Buy a used computer.
It will inevitably have an incurable virus or contain subversive files that will attract the attention of the government.

### Buy a watch on the street.
That "Rolex" will work fine for forty-eight hours and then you will discover there is nothing inside of it except a rubber band.

### Buy bulk food from a warehouse store.
You had better not be able to finish a ten-pound jar of mayonnaise before it goes bad.

### Contemplate the meaning of life.
Trying to figure out why you or anything at all exists is even more futile than trying to figure out why Wayne Newton has remained consistently popular over the years.

### Drill for oil in your backyard.
Although it's unlikely that you will find enough oil in your backyard to make it financially worthwhile, you may discover some power lines the electric company has been looking for.

### Drive cross-country with the kids.
A stupid thing that has messed up parents' lives since the invention of the car. When your daughter throws up on your son about ten miles out of town, you'll begin to regret you didn't fly.

**Eat creatures that crawl on the bottom of the sea.**
Lobsters, crabs, and their crustacean cousins are not food but aquatic Dustbusters. If you are what you eat, when you eat seafood you're seacrap.

**Eat Olestra.**
I personally avoid anything that adds to the likelihood of anal leakage.

**Go to a country where it is advised to take a pint of your own blood.**
This is not a normal "packing hint."

**Go to a restaurant whose name you can't pronounce.**
This means they are trying way too hard. The simpler the name, the better the food.

**Have a caricature of yourself done.**
Actually wanting some yahoo to exaggerate your worst feature or features and then document it for perpetuity means you have bigger problems than just bad taste in art.

**Hire a lawyer named Skeech, Frenchy, or Cookie.**
If you're looking for a bouncer or pool shark, however, you've got your man.

**Join the reserves.**
One day you are running through the woods with a bunch of buddies, and the next day you're in a sand bunker in the Mideast dodging SCUD missiles.

**Make a robot.**
Everyone knows that all robots will eventually go haywire and try to kill their masters.

**Own a moat.**
Besides the fact that home security systems have advanced considerably, your neighbors are apt to misinterpret your moat as a sign of standoffishness.

**Repair your roof yourself.**
You'll be lucky if you don't kill yourself just by climbing that stack of rotted wood you call a ladder.

**Revise history.**
Columbus was not an imperialist monster. He was just a guy looking for spices and got lost probably because he refused to ask for directions.

**Send a chain letter.**
No misfortune will come to you if you do not send a chain letter to ten other people. In fact, passing on this stupidity to ten other people will make ten more people hate you.

**Send your child to boarding school.**
Boarding school won't make your child a better person through discipline, but it will equip him to be a much better juvenile delinquent. Avoid any schools, in fact, whose ads include either a picture of someone in uniform or a horse.

**Sleep with a hotel bedspread.**
If you knew what was still on it, you would never sleep with one or even stay in a hotel again.

**Take a Rorschach test.**
A useless psychological tool which some of my colleagues would have you believe reveals special insight into one's personality. So what if

someone thinks that all inkblots look like a female spider eating her mate?

## Take a vow of celibacy.
Just because you can't get a date doesn't mean you should turn it into a cause. Your urge for sex will manifest itself in even stranger ways.

## Take a vow of silence.
Although we'd all appreciate this a great deal, it is unhealthy for a person to keep all of his thoughts to himself, especially if that person is you.

## Trace your genealogy.
You will be disappointed to discover that most of the leaves on your family tree were ne'er-do-wells who spent most of their lives in debtor's prison and avoided being sent to Australia only by dying of gonorrhea.

## Use leeches for any purposes other than fishing.
It's bad enough that you have leeches in your possession at all. If you haven't heard, by the way, bloodletting turned out to be not such a good idea.

**Wear armor.**
Not only heavy and bulky but totally ineffective against all weapons except swords and jousting poles.

**Wear magnets.**
They won't heal your bursitis, but they do make a handy place to keep paper clips.

**Work for a boss.**
Ants, not people, are here to take orders from someone else. Find a job in which you can fulfill your dreams, no matter how stupid they probably are.

# 17

# Stupid Jobs

Because who you are in America has much to do with what you do professionally, choosing the right career path is of utmost importance. Unfortunately, many people end up in degrading, dangerous, or otherwise less than fulfilling occupations, and this serves as a major source of regret, frustration, and general angst. So you don't end up as an anonymous drone in the hive of life, here are some stupid jobs that you should avoid at all costs.

## Be a chimney sweep.
Reality check: You are not in a charming Mary Poppins movie. You are in real life, and you've got a stupid job. Find an occupation that does not involve scrubbing soot and removing dead critters out of chimneys.

**Be a coal miner.**
If you lived in a mining community decades ago, you probably had few career alternatives. Today, however, you have options. You can be a strip miner!

**Be a crash test dummy.**
Larry and Vince pretty much have this one covered.

**Be a fishwife.**
Being a woman who sells fish may have once garnered some status, but today you'll just be known as the woman who smells funny.

**Be a picador.**
Stabbing a bull to piss him off even more is no way to make a living, *mi amigo*.

**Be an alchemist.**
Turning base metals into gold will probably be more financially rewarding than your office job, but you will miss chatting it up with the gang at the watercooler.

**Be an indentured servant.**
Avoid long-term contracts that deed you to another person.

## Be a referee or umpire.

You're constantly abused, look ridiculous, and occasionally get hit on the head. Good news: You are not a flight attendant. Bad news: You're an adult who wears stripes to work.

## Be a repo man.

Repossessing automobiles and appliances from people who would really like to keep them may expose you to situations you're not prepared for. Saving a twenty-six-inch television from unwarranted usage just isn't worth it.

## Be a security guard.

Ninety-nine percent of the time you will be totally bored while the remaining 1 percent you will be in danger. This makes this a 100 percent stupid job.

## Be a shepherd.

You will become much too familiar with certain members of your herd and find yourself involved in complicated romantic triangles. Take a job in which it will be easier to maintain a professional relationship with your colleagues.

## Be a telemarketer.
A rare combination of low wages, low status, and little or no contribution toward society. I'm taking a flyer on this, but selling siding on the phone is probably not what you thought you'd be doing when you were a kid.

## Drive a taxi.
It has always puzzled me why people who are newest to this country and are thus least familiar with directions are put in charge of driving the rest of us around.

## Quit your job before having another.
Your savings will dry up much faster than you thought they would, and you will learn that Kraft makes seven different varieties of macaroni and cheese.

## Sell anything door-to-door.
Nobody wants to buy an encyclopedia, brush, or Bible anymore, particularly from some stranger who wants to hang out in their living room for a while.

### Sell Herbalife.
You are not bringing good health to the masses. You are part of a crappy pyramid scheme selling products to people who don't really want them.

### Substitute teach.
Substitute teachers exist purely to receive heaps of abuse that children cannot give to their regular teachers because they know they will see their regular teachers the following day.

### Temp.
Temps exist only because people with real jobs would never do the kind of work that temps are hired to do. Choose a job that does not involve being surprised where you're going to work that day and what you're going to do.

### Tend bar.
You'll be working in an environment that exists solely so people can exchange reality for an illusory state of well-being. Dispensing beverages that make people do and say things they normally wouldn't do is not really making the world a better place.

**Wear a paper hat at work.**
Unless you're a doctor, this is going to involve deep fat fryers at some point.

**Work for a nonprofit organization.**
Career tip for you do-gooders: "Nonprofit" means "loser" in a capitalist society.

**Write books.**
You call this a living? Choose a career in which you don't have to remind people that there are more than five hundred stupid things they can do to mess up their lives.

# 18

# Stupid Lifestyles

In our pursuit of the answers to the big questions of life we sometimes end up traveling on some unusual and truly stupid paths. I am not opposed to your trying out new and different things, but if you find that you have given all your earthly possessions to on organization that tells you when you may or may not urinate, you have probably chosen a stupid lifestyle. Here are some other lifestyle choices that are cause for alarm, if not intervention, should you find yourself living one.

## Be a drifter and/or a grifter.
Roaming the countryside with no real purpose except to drift and/or grift is a perfect example of why you're such an underachiever.

## Be a hobo.
Who doesn't like to travel? You may grow weary, however, of sleeping in boxcars and carrying all your clothes on a stick.

### Be known in your neighborhood as "the cat lady."

If there are more cats in your house or apartment than bedrooms, you are a candidate for this dubious title. Find homes for the critters before the authorities come and raze your house.

### Be referred to as a "ne'er-do-well."

In case you don't know what this means, it implies that you never do well.

### Drive a large pickup or sports utility vehicle.

Apparently everyone but you knows this obviously means you have a tiny penis. Get rid of that two-ton phallic symbol if you're wondering why everyone is laughing and pointing at you.

### Forage for food.

Eating off the lay of the land was perfectly appropriate for certain native cultures in preindustrial times but now is cause for concern. Lay off the bark and berries and get some food that comes in unnatural packaging.

### Get labeled as a "loner."

Loners account for 98.5 percent of the crimes in this country that make absolutely no sense at all.

**Go incognito.**
You know you have messed up your life when you can no longer be the person you are.

**Go to a bar where everyone knows your name.**
This does not mean that you are a popular person. This means that you are probably an alcoholic.

**Hibernate.**
If you're sleeping for months at a time during the winter, you are officially hibernating. Take this seriously, particularly if you have developed an extreme fondness for honey.

**Hire a *feng shui* expert.**
Call me and I'll be happy to move your sofa a foot to the left, too, for one hundred dollars an hour.

**Hire a personal coach.**
People who need other people to guide their lives need something more than a personal coach. They need a brain transplant.

## Join a commune.

Living together in perfect harmony is a great idea, but the fact is you're going to get really pissed at Brother Tad when he eats the Froot Loops you thought you'd hid pretty darn well.

## Kill time.

So you are given a finite amount of time to achieve your dreams, fall in love, and live life to the fullest, and you are looking for ways to make the time go faster? Consider every precious second you have an opportunity to realize your full mediocrity.

## Lead a double life.

Having two families in two cities qualifies here, as does going out at night to cruise for young men named 'Derek' or 'Todd.'

## Live in a gated community.

Just because you're a Have sequestering yourself in a private, gated community from the Have Nots doesn't mean you're any happier or less stupid than they are. It only means you can afford a really good fence and a fat security guard named Wally.

**Live in a lighthouse.**
Very romantic from the outside but that damn light will keep you up all night.

**Live in a van down by the river.**
You are one notch below the untouchable caste of American society, making you not only untouchable but unlookable.

**Move to a small town.**
They sound romantic but are more like *Peyton Place* than *Mayberry R.F.D.* You will long for Pad Thai and those amazing smoothies made with fresh raspberries.

**Retire before the age of sixty.**
Golf, mah-jongg, and waxing your car are barely fun when you don't have the time to do them. Keep working unless you really enjoy meaningless activities that take a long time to complete.

**Room with anyone who knows all the lyrics to all of Styx's songs.**
It is probably harmless, but you never know.

**Run with the wolves.**
Women who metaphorically run with the wolves to get in touch with their inner warrior fail to recognize that being a warrior is inappropriate in every situation, except in a state of declared war.

**Sleep on a water bed.**
Water beds are a product of an era when everything alternative and experimental was viewed as good. Now we know that they make you nauseated, and the only people that own them are old hippies and sluts.

# 19

# Stupid Looks

Do you often look up to find people staring at you? Have you ever been asked to be photographed for a "before" picture in an ad? Are you often mistaken for a tree or other inanimate object? While you can't totally control what you look like, there are steps you can take to improve your appearance and make you a happier, more confident person. Before laws are passed making intentional ugliness a crime, get familiar with these kinds of stupid looks.

## Be mistaken for a homeless person.
You have apparently pushed the envelope of vintage clothes a smidge too far. Do the right thing and return the change you have been given by a passerby.

## Cut your own hair.
Even professional haircutters do not attempt to cut their own hair because they know it can only result in wrestler hair or some sort of mutant version.

**Dye your hair any color that does not occur in nature.**
Dyeing your hair neon orange might have been interesting in 1980, but now it just makes you look like you've been overdoing it on the beta-carotene.

**Get a perm.**
The smell alone should tell you that this is a stupid thing to do to your hair. The other thing that should tell you is that no one looks good with one.

**Get an instant tan.**
Instant tanning lotions make you look like the color of Crayolas everyone wanted to get rid of, while tanning booths are known to cook your insides.

**Get your colors done.**
You are not a Spring or Summer. You are not a Fall or Winter. You are a huge sucker who just bought one hundred dollars worth of something that will give you a rash.

**Have breast implants.**
You were simply not intended to have breasts as big and hard as bowling balls, even if you do live in Los Angeles.

## Have cosmetic surgery.

Having elective surgery to make some part of your body larger, smaller, or smoother is a clear sign of your need to conform to social norms regarding appearance. Keep your unique features even if you do look remarkably like Alfred E. Newman.

## Model your figure after Barbie's.

A human body that is proportional to Barbie's would make Xena the Warrior Princess look like Kate Moss. I don't think you want a 56-18-36 figure.

## Pierce an extremity.

People who put holes in especially sensitive parts of their bodies make me wonder if we all crawled out of the same primordial ooze.

## Take more than fifteen minutes to do your hair.

If it takes any longer, the issue is not your hair. Figure out what personality or physical flaw you are overcompensating for by having oversized hair.

**Try to lose weight any other way than eating less food.**

It's really this simple: Getting smaller means you have to put fewer things inside you.

**Wear a bib.**

Stupid-looking even when eating lobster. Extremely stupid-looking in most social settings not involving food.

**Wear a bola tie.**

You don't look like some Western stud who just rode in on a horse. You look like a twit who inexplicably has shoestrings running down your shirt.

**Wear a cape.**

Capes are for superheroes and viscounts, neither of which exist in society as we know it. Put away the cape before someone mistakes you for a vampire and drives a stake through your heart.

**Wear a crown.**

Even the queen of England looks like she's playing dress-up when wearing a crown. Wearing a crown or tiara makes you look less like royalty, more like you've won a beauty pageant.

**Wear a dog collar.**
Pet accessories just don't translate well to humans. Try a look that doesn't make you look like you're owned by a more evolved species.

**Wear a medallion.**
Unless it is from the Olympics, you should have stopped wearing it around the time Nixon resigned.

**Wear a monocle.**
The Colonel Klink look may have worked for Nazi prisoner-of-war camp commandants, but for others it just makes people think you've lost half your glasses.

**Wear a muumuu.**
Since muumuus are designed for people who weigh three hundred pounds, it's not so much that you're wearing a muumuu as the fact that you weigh three hundred pounds.

**Wear a toupee.**
Do you really need to broadcast to the world that you are so self-conscious about your lack of hair that you are willing to appear as if you had a ferret on top of your head?

**Wear an eye patch simply for effect.**
This worked great for the Arrow Shirt Man but that was like forty
years ago and he wasn't real. Rather than making you look
distinguished, wearing an eye patch today just makes you look like
you're a poor insurance risk.

**Wear chaps.**
Fur was never intended to be worn below the waist.

**Wear clogs.**
Let's all agree to think of Holland for cheese instead of footwear, shall
we? Take off those ergonomic disasters and put on some shoes that
are preferably not made of wood.

**Wear Dockers.**
Why not just stamp your forehead ORDINARY GUY WHO LIVES IN THE
'BURBS?

**Wear facial hair.**
For men, wearing facial hair begs the question, "What are you
covering up?" For women, wearing facial hair begs the question,
"Have you noticed that very few other women are wearing facial
hair?"

## Wear more than a modicum of makeup.

It is no coincidence that a woman who uses pancake makeup will look very much like a pancake.

## Wear overalls.

Unless you are a tyke or a farmer, this is not an attractive look. Try to wear pants that don't extend over your shoulders and wear clothing in general that doesn't instantly bring to mind characters from *Hee-Haw*.

# 20

# Stupid Mistakes

Of all the stupid things people do to mess up their lives, stupid mistakes are unquestionably the stupidest. Errors in judgment or normal slipups are one thing, but regular, major screwups are a sign of deep psychological distress. You could be, as Freud would argue, sabotaging yourself out of a fear of success or, as Dr. Larry would argue, just a bonehead. So the word *regret* doesn't become an even larger part of your vocabulary, remember to dodge these stupid bullets.

**Admit you were in jail.**
Don't jeopardize your future for mistakes made in your past. Present that missing year on your résumé as a "Criminal Justice System Fellowship."

**Attend a high school reunion.**
You will realize your high school years were not a positive, character-building experience but rather four years at Beavis & Butthead Central.

## Bullshit bullshitters.

Lying to better liars can only get you into more trouble.

## Burn bridges.

The person you least expected to ever see again after calling him a single-cell organism will be the very same person who will be interviewing you three years later for a job you really want and need.

## Flash a gang sign.

For better or worse, consciously or unconsciously sending a message to gang members will probably be the last stupid thing you do to mess up your life.

## Fool Mother Nature.

If Mother Nature gets pissed off about margarine, she is definitely not going to be pleased about bigger offenses against nature. NutraSweet must have sent her into a hyperkinetic sugar fit.

## Get hypnotized.

I don't care what they tell you. One day you will be at a party and someone will unintentionally say the magic word, and you will be clucking like a chicken or quacking like a duck. If this is normally what you do at party, never mind.

## Have your stomach stapled.
Internal organs do not like to be touched by office equipment.

## Hire contractors named Moe, Larry, and Curly.
Dollars to doughnuts you will come home to find your plumbing, wallpaper, or landscaping really screwed up. Look out for this crazy painter named Shemp as well.

## Ignore the information revolution.
The cybertrain has left the station, and you better get on board before you become even more of a fossil.

## Invade Kuwait.
The United States government is just going to kick your ass back to where you came from, so don't waste your time.

## Leave it to Beaver.
Should you really trust anything to anyone named Beaver?

## Over do it on the fertility drugs.
When they kick in all at once, you'll be getting diapers donated to you for life after all the publicity.

## Pose nude for your boyfriend.

Those pictures will be flying through cyberspace at warp speed the day after you break up. Also refuse his suggestion to videotape yourselves having sex or else have fun visiting your own personal website called www.fillinyournameherehavingsex.com.

## Put your eye out.

Sharp objects and projectiles present a clear and present danger, in case you haven't heard. Special attention should be paid to hot pokers.

## Send in a warranty form.

They don't want to guarantee your product as much as they want to know everything about you so they can sell you or your demographic clone something equally useless.

## Sign a contract without reading it.

Although no doubt true, claiming ignorance and stupidity is something the courts are allowing for less and less.

## Sue a lawyer.

Are you completely nuts? Suing someone who has unlimited time to make your life a litigious hell is akin to repeatedly hitting yourself on the head with a two-by-four.

## Take other people's prescriptions.

The drug that works perfectly well for your friend may have a totally different effect for you. Stop taking everything if you notice hair appearing on body parts that have never grown hair before.

## Travel to any place in which a bodyguard is recommended.

There are enough things to worry about while travelling without fear of assassination by the Russian mafia, highway bandidos, or the local police.

## Use a chain saw.

Chain saws should be used only by lumberjacks and psychos in B movies.

## Vacation anyplace where you're told not to leave the hotel.

Why would anyone voluntarily travel thousands of miles to a hotel that looks just like the Marriott downtown, except you can't leave this one because you'll probably be kidnapped?

**Wear a thong bikini.**
A mistake unless you belong to the .00001 percent of the population who are leggy supermodels, in which case I couldn't recommend it more strongly.

**Work overtime without getting paid.**
Overtime is your opportunity to charge much higher rates for much worse work. Don't stay a minute extra unless it's for time-and-a-half and credit for expensive meals you would never buy on your own dime.

## 21

# Stupid Risks

Do you take unnecessary risks purely for the thrill? Or do you have a self-destructive streak, continually pushing the risk envelope by placing yourself in increasingly dangerous situations? Either way, the odds will eventually catch up with you, and you will suffer the consequences of your bold yet incredibly stupid ways. Don't take these kind of stupid risks unless you want to further tempt the fate gods who are already clearly not on your side.

### Be a hero or heroine.
There are plenty of brave, foolish people who are just waiting for the chance to risk life and limb to catch the bad guy. Do the right thing and let 'em.

### Be a human fly.
Scaling buildings will get you the attention you're yearning for, but will it get you the happiness you also seek?

**Be a martyr.**
Yeah, you saved the day but now you're dead. Live to tell about it is
what I say.

**Be a mercenary.**
Killing people you don't know for money makes plain old murder
seem almost justified. I'd pass if "anonymous homicide" appears in the
job responsibilities.

**Be a scab.**
Performing a job for a wage that people already know is less than it
should be is stupid. Plus you're going to get yelled at and have eggs
and rotten fruit thrown at you.

**Become a bounty hunter.**
Chasing down the dregs of society is no job for a mensch like you.
Go back to your nice job selling shoes at the mall.

**Buy fireworks.**
A klutz like you should not be in possession of a Swiss Army knife,
much less explosives.

## Challenge someone to a duel.

Your honor has been called into question and now you feel you must defend it with swords or pistols at dawn. What you're forgetting is that you've got a most excellent lawyer who can sue big-time for libel or slander.

## Defy gravity.

Gravity is one of those firm rules of the universe with which you cannot negotiate. Avoid situations likely to lead to falling to the earth at rapid speed.

## Defy the time-space continuum.

Like gravity, time and space are pretty much nonnegotiable. Going back or ahead in time or taking up space that is already occupied can only mess up your life.

## Eat wild mushrooms.

Any time you pick and eat wild mushrooms there is a relatively good chance you will either die or begin to see a world very much like that depicted in "Yellow Submarine."

## Have no alibi.

Whether you did whatever you're accused of or not, you should always have a set of potential alibis to get you off the hook. Keep a list on your person at all times just in case.

## Hitchhike.

This form of transportation has been a stupid idea since the counterculture crashed and burned in 1968. Do so now and there's a fifty-fifty chance you will either become a sex slave or be eaten.

## Join a cabal or cartel.

I don't know what these organizations are exactly, but I do know they usually involve scary-looking Arabs. If you choose to plot secretly, conspire, or try to control the world's supply of oil, do so at your own risk.

## Keep a pet snake.

At best you have a pet that makes most people feel very uncomfortable. At worst you have a pet that will wrap itself around your neck while you sleep and will then swallow you whole.

## Make a bomb in your basement.
One day you'll go a bit too heavy on the ammonium chloride and your remains, which now consist of a piece of your little toe, will be buried in an Altoids tin.

## Operate farm machinery while on medication.
This instruction is wisely on the label of any drug that will give you a good buzz. I coendorse the idea that driving a thresher while thinking you're Jim Morrison is not recommended.

## Own a howitzer.
Lord knows a long-range missile launcher can certainly come in handy at times, but do you really need to own one? I would lease before making such a sizable investment.

## Perform surgery on yourself.
This is more difficult than it looks, particularly after general anesthesia. Be a sport and let the professional rebuild your bum knee.

## Play chicken.
Winning a game of chicken is not a sign of bravery but a sign that you take pride in being more stupid than the average moron.

## Send lawyers, guns, and money.

You apparently know someone personally involved in a revolution. Instead of sending these things, do your friend a big favor and tell your friend to get the hell out.

## Swim with the sharks.

Despite what any business guru may tell you, I just can't see how this is possible without getting eaten alive.

# 22

# Stupid Romance

When bitten by the love bug, people tend to make a beeline directly to Stupidville. The precious little amount of common sense of your average guy or gal immediately evaporates once he or she becomes smitten, creating a bevy of dicey, potentially horribly embarrassing scenarios. Do not succumb to these stupid romantic things or learn to live with a perpetually broken heart or the sex life of a heterosexual Benedictine monk.

## Answer a personal ad.
That "good-looking SWM" is going to be a spitting-image lookalike of Barney Frank and that "disease-free, financially secure DWF" is bound to also have a restraining order against having any contact with her ex-husband.

## Break up in a public place.
Your strategy to break up in a public place to avoid a scene will backfire on you. Be prepared for widescale slapping of the face and tossing of beverages.

**Bring a past, present, or future lover along on a date.**
I believe this is precisely the situation in which the question "What the hell were you thinking?" was originally coined.

**Consider your letter-writing relationship with the prison inmate to be one of "committed monogamy."**
Committed monogamy is indeed a sign of maturity, but you may want to consider having a relationship with someone within the 99 percent of the population that is not incarcerated.

**Covet your neighbor.**
Even a bird knows not to foul its nest, and its brain is even smaller than yours. Covet someone from across town if you absolutely have to covet.

**Fake orgasms.**
No one benefits from the deceit of deceits. Put up or shut up.

**Fall asleep during sex.**
Falling asleep during the most intimate, intense thing people can do together is something your partner may take very personally. Remain conscious or risk giving it away that you'd rather be dreaming that you're hitting a three-point shot with one second left in the big game.

**Get dumped.**
Does Dr. Larry really have to tell you that it is infinitely better to be the dumper versus the dumpee? Move fast when you see the breakup winds a'blowin'.

**Get or give a hickey.**
You felt stupid about this when you were thirteen, and you will feel even more stupid now. Worst of all, you will have to wear a turtleneck, an article of clothing that looks good only after you've been skiing.

**Go on a blind date with anyone described as "cute."**
"Cute" is a euphemism for coyote ugly, as if you didn't know that already.

**Go on a blind date with anyone described as having a "great personality."**
"Great personality" is code for "shops at House of Large Sizes."

**Go on a blind date with anyone with a "cute personality."**
Run for the hills.

**Have a crush on a gay person if you're straight.**
I'm sure you're very nice, but there is no way in hell that this person will ever want to see you naked.

**Have a crush on a straight person if you're gay.**
Ditto.

**Have a long-distance relationship.**
So there are hundreds, thousands, or perhaps millions of perfectly eligible people in your town and you choose someone who lives in another time zone. Do not mistake a pen pal for a relationship.

**Have a sugar daddy.**
If you want to call him a sugar daddy, that's fine. Be aware, however, that other people refer to the exchange of sex for financial gain in different terms.

**Leave your partner for someone you met over the Internet.**
That cutie named Sasha is really a three-hundred-pound truck driver named Roger with sexual identity issues. Walk away from the computer slowly and confront the hard truth that is reality.

**Make out with your boss.**
You will never be able to take your boss totally seriously again after having your tongue in his or her mouth.

**Make out with your subordinate.**
Start looking for another job and a lawyer. Actually, I'd start looking for the lawyer first.

**Marry the same person twice.**
It is a myth that lightning can't strike the same place twice. Marrying the same person again allows you the unique opportunity to inherit baggage from a previous relationship while simultaneously creating new baggage.

**Own a plastic woman for any reason whatsoever.**
You're a big fat liar if you tell me you practice CPR on it. Or should I say her.

**Participate in any form of cybersex.**
I don't know about you, but I've got this thing where I like to at least be in the same room as my partner when I'm having sex.

**Play hard to get.**
This will reduce your chances of finding a mate to a microscopic degree. Given your track record, you should play as easy to get as possible.

**Sign a prenuptial agreement.**
Because it's just a question of when you'll start hating each other, waiving your right to one-half of your intended's goodies is legal suicide. Share and share alike is what I say, especially if your dreamboat is loaded.

**Take a date to a topless joint.**
Nonmorons go to dinner and/or a movie on dates, I guess I have to inform you.

**Use the rhythm method.**
This has worked wonderfully well for all those Irish Catholics with small families.

# 23

# Stupid Spirituality

Can any form of spirituality really be considered stupid? Oh yes, ye of stupid faith. Just like anything else, there is the stupid and the nonstupid, and it is your responsibility to move as close as you possibly can to the nonstupid side of the fence. Don't fall into these stupid spiritual traps lest your soul be consigned to the purgatory of eternal stupidity.

## Become a druid.
I understand how you think being a Celtic prophet or sorcerer can help you win friends and influence people. What you haven't considered, however, is that by being one you're being a total dolt.

## Become a heretic.
Heretics have generally not had a happy go of it throughout history. Just nod up and down if a group of angry townspeople pound on your door and ask if you believe that there is an all knowing, all-powerful ruler of the universe.

## Become a missionary.

God has not instructed you to spread the gospel. Admit that you want fewer heathens in the world only because you want more people just like you.

## Become a monk.

Dedicating yourself to a life of asceticism is admirable, but keep in mind that we're all going to be out here eating Snickerdoodles and watching *Nick at Nite* while you're eating gruel and pondering the infinite wisdom of the Almighty.

## Become a nun.

Yes, your sex life will improve dramatically, but there is more to life than sex, isn't there? Choose a career less likely to lead to romantic encounters, like being a masseuse at an all-male college.

## Call a psychic hotline.

They do not know your future. They do not know your past. They do know, however, that dimwits like you will pay good money to hear them talk.

## Call yourself a shaman or healer.

You have about as much ability to heal the sick as a pastry. Quit going around talking about chakras and figure out why you need to play God.

## Channel anyone or anything.

Channeling is the art of being a vehicle or voice for another spirit. Just an observation: Any spirit worth its metaphysical salt would probably not want anything to do with you, living or dead.

## Chant.

Repeating monosyllabic utterances only makes primates look that much more intelligent than you.

## Dabble in the occult.

You are fortunate the occult does not exist, or by now you would have been turned into an amphibian or reptile by a much superior being from the dark side.

## Expect reincarnation.

Don't know about you, but I'm betting my chips on this life versus some next one where my soul magically takes root in a higher, evolved being.

**Find God.**
One day you're a normal person, and the next day you're confusing mythology for reality. Snap out of it.

**Join a cult.**
Do I really need to articulate the issues associated with joining an organization led by a charismatic figure believing a spaceship will soon whisk you all off to paradise?

**Practice voodoo.**
The only pain resulting from sticking pins in figures that look like people will be that which occurs when you stab yourself. If causing pain to others was as easy as voodoo practitioners would have you believe, there would be a House of Voodoo next to every Starbucks.

**Search for the Holy Grail.**
Setting off on a quest to find a particular drinking vessel, regardless of how special may be, seems to me to be kind of an odd thing to want to do.

**See the Virgin Mary.**
The Virgin Mary has better things to do than make herself seen by you, especially in the form of a burrito.

## Take religion too seriously.

Tell me otherwise when you have any evidence at all suggesting we are more than biological flotsam and jetsam hurtling through a random, meaningless universe.

## Try to bring back the dead.

The dead will come back when and where they like and not because you ask them to while you and your pals are sitting around your kitchen table in the dark.

## Visit a psychic.

They have as much extrasensory perception as a potato. Buy a Magic 8-Ball and save twenty bucks.

## Visit the Dalai Lama.

You'll schlep halfway around the world to find a fat guy in an orange suit. When the Beatles visited him in 1967, they were very disappointed that the only remarkable thing about him was his uncanny resemblance to Mama Cass.

**Wear a crystal.**
The only impact crystals will have on your personality is their ability to let everyone know that you're a superstitious flake who believes a rock controls your life.

**Worship an idol.**
If you were God, would you take the form of something that would be marked "as is" at a yard sale?

# 24

# Stupid Tastes

A simple explanation for your messed-up life could be that you have stupid tastes. Through no fault of your own, your aesthetic sense perhaps never developed, serving as a vivid reminder to the rest of the world that you are a man or woman of remarkably stupid tastes. Stop exhibiting these kind of stupid sensibilities if you want to be viewed as a person who does not belong to the Clampett family.

**Burn incense.**
Incense exists only because it is the only thing that stinks more than pot. Unless you're in a dorm room with a towel under the door, leave the incense to bizarre religious rituals.

**Drink decaf.**
Drinking decaffeinated coffee is like kissing your sister.

**Drink light beer.**
Drinking light beer is like kissing your aunt.

### Drink Tang.
And the reason a nonastronaut would choose to drink powdered orange juice versus real orange juice would be . . . ?

### Drink 3.2 beer.
Three-point-two beer exists only to prevent you and your hooligan buddies from getting even rowdier than normal at ballgames. Drink it only if you enjoy feeling bloated or like to pee in a trough every two innings.

### Drink wine from Canada.
Canada has produced very few memorable things, and wine is one of the least memorable.

### Eat at any theme restaurant.
Eating anyplace where the decor takes precedence over the food is chock-full of stupidity. And Bon Jovi never even touched that guitar.

### Eat food on a stick.
Putting food on a stick is a cheap attempt to add entertainment value to bad food. Eating food on a stick anywhere other than a state fair is an insult to whatever animal has ended up on the short end of that stick.

**Eat vittles.**
Being raised in a rural environment does not give you the right to eat "vittles." Quit eating them and start eating "food" like the rest of us who live outside the town limits of Bumblefuck.

**Fly a decorative flag.**
A scourge on our cultural landscape and an irksome one since there is, the last time I checked, no nation state dedicated to the ideals of bunnies, ducks, or jack-o'-lanterns.

**Follow trends.**
There is nothing sadder than someone who believes doing whatever is temporarily popular will make him temporarily popular.

**Hire a personal shopper.**
So you're conceding you have no aesthetic sense at all and must rely on someone else to choose your clothes. Can you say, "Mommy"?

**Imitate Martha Stewart.**
The smart money has it that she's not human at all but rather a cyborg waiting for the proper moment to take over the earth.

## Install shag carpeting.

Carpet fibers longer than one inch are sensibly outlawed in most states except certain parts of New Jersey. Rust- and avocado-colored shag carpeting, thankfully, has been banned by both the EPA and OSHA.

## Keep gnomes, fairies, or elves on your lawn.

This is perfectly fair justification for an attack on Earth from outer space.

## Keep old cars in your yard.

This is cultural shorthand for "white trash." Keeping old appliances in your yard, on the other hand, means "relatives of white trash."

## Live in a trailer park.

Besides being the unofficial untouchable caste of society, one day you will notice that your home is flying rapidly toward another county. Live in a place that does not become aloft on windy days.

## Mistake your furniture for being "shabby chic" furniture when it is actually "pure crap."

If there's any doubt, it's definitely the latter.

**Nominate any song by Foreigner or Journey as you and your partner's song.**
It's bad enough that R.E.O. Speedwagon was your favorite band from 1977 to 1979. Don't bring any more bad vibes into your relationship than exist naturally.

**Order food off a menu by its number.**
Just going to a restaurant that assigns numbers to its food items is a little troubling. Cooperating with this unseemly practice by referring to food by a number implies that you appreciate your meal coming off an assembly line like a Geo Prizm.

**Patronize Hooters.**
Do not encourage these people.

**Put a knit sweater or hat on a dog.**
This is cruel and unusual punishment, and you should be arrested for it.

**Put out potpourri.**
One of the most curious paradoxes of American life is the popularity of potpourri despite the fact that no one can stand the smell of it.

**Read the tabloids.**
Even pretending for entertainment purposes that a baby ate its own
foot while stuck in a refrigerator is something you should not go along
with.

**Reckon.**
Real people think. People from towns named Squirrel Holler or
Hootersville reckon.

**Smoke generic cigarettes.**
Smoking is disgusting enough without you being so addicted to tar
and nicotine that you're willing to declare to the world that you don't
even care which brand you smoke.

**Wear a fanny pack.**
Wearing a fanny pack within the United States is cultural code for
"can't pack personal belongings into pants because of big fanny."
Wearing a fanny pack abroad is why everyone who lives outside the
United States hates us.

**Wear acrylic clothing.**
Acrylic and all petrochemically based clothing are justifiably
flammable.

**Wear anything with beads or rhinestones.**
Considered gauche unless you're prepared to sing about dogs, pickups, trains, or any combination thereof.

**Wear feathers before sundown.**
A fashion faux pas if there ever was one.

**Wear latex.**
Overdoing it with latex is a fashion trap we all fall into once in a while. Limit your latex accessorizing to gloves, condoms, and the occasional sweater.

# 25

# Stupid Vices

How fitting that *563 Stupid Things People Do to Mess Up Their Lives* concludes with stupid vices. Despite having twenty years of experience in the psychiatry game, I am still amazed by some of my patients' compulsions to alter their state of mind with foreign substances or to participate in stupid sexual encounters. Abstain from these kind of stupid vices or face the consequences that come with hedonism run amok.

## Be a crack whore.
Significantly stupider than merely being a whore. If you're going to sell your body, try to use the proceeds for nonaddictive goods or services.

## Carry a flask.
Flasks were very cool in the 1920s because it was the era of prohibition. Today, I guess I have to inform you, drinking is legal, which makes concealing a flask a curious if not disquieting habit.

**Do a threesome.**
A common fantasy but one you will regret when your partner ends up enjoying sex much more with the third party than he or she ever did with you.

**Download porn.**
Each time you log onto a pornographic web site you are announcing to the world that you seek vicarious sex because you can't get laid. You will also soon be receiving sex toys in the mail that are free for thirty days.

**Drink moonshine.**
People who choose to drink homemade alcohol deserve to go blind, crazy, or both. Come down from the hills and try a beverage that doesn't double as paint thinner.

**Engage in kinky sex.**
Sex should not require any more apparatus than standard-issued equipment. Put the implements of torture or forcible restraint away, or you will get caught up in a perpetually escalating spiral of kinkalia.

**Get drunk at your office party.**
I think you'll regret photocopying your butt and faxing the lovely image to the entire sales force.

**Not remember how you got home.**
Even after a few drinks you should recall the basic form of transportation that delivered you to your door.

**Own a bong.**
It's 2000. Do you know where your mind is? Retire the bong to your extensive "Bad Habits of the Early 1970s" file.

**Pay for a hooker with a check when you're the mayor of Cincinnati.**
This will get you forced out of politics and into hosting tawdry talk shows.

**Pay for sex.**
Sex is not a commodity that should be purchased like a pair of shoes but rather a special event shared between two people. Unless, of course, your best buddy is getting married, and he already has a DVD player.

## Swap partners.
This always seems like it will be a lot of fun but has in fact led to disaster every time it has occurred in history. Dance with the one who brung ya.

## Waste away (again) in Margaritaville.
Spending your time looking for a lost shaker of salt is what I call time better spent doing something else. I would claim that there's a woman to blame.